This Planner Belongs To :

_____

Printed by CreateSpace, An Amazon.com Company
A Publication by Jada Correia

Success Doesn't Just Happen It's Planned For.

Monthly Budget

Income		
Income 1		
Income 2		
Other Income		
TOTAL INCOME		

Expenses

Month :

Budget :

Bill To Be Paid	Date Due	Amount	Paid	Note
			◯	
			◯	
			◯	
			◯	
			◯	
			◯	
			◯	
			◯	
			◯	
			◯	
			◯	
			◯	
			◯	
			◯	
			◯	
			◯	
			◯	
			◯	
			◯	
TOTAL				

Monthly Budget

Other Expenses	Date	Amount	Note
TOTAL			

TOTAL INCOME

TOTAL EXPENSES

DIFFERENCE

Notes

_____

_____

_____

_____

_____

Weekly Expense Tracker

Month : March   Week Of :   Budget : 2,000

Monday   Date ..../......./.......

Description	Amount
Nails	$80
groceries	$200
Total	

Tuesday   Date ..../......./.......

Description	Amount
Teeth	$230
gas	$35
Total	

Wednesday   Date ..../......./.......

Description	Amount
Total	

Thursday   Date ..../......./.......

Description	Amount
Lashes	$150
gas	$20
Total	

Weekly Expense Tracker

Total Expenses :   **Balance :**

Friday   Date ..../......./.......

Description	Amount
Tooth gem	$20-40
Tat?	$100-200
gas	$20
Total	

Saturday   Date ..../......./.......

Description	Amount
Total	

Sunday   Date ..../......./.......

Description	Amount
Total	

Notes

Weekly Expense Tracker

Month :   Week Of :   Budget :

Monday   Date ..../......./.......

Description	Amount
Total	

Tuesday   Date ..../......./.......

Description	Amount
Total	

Wednesday   Date ..../......./.......

Description	Amount
Total	

Thursday   Date ..../......./.......

Description	Amount
Total	

Weekly Expense Tracker

Total Expenses :   **Balance :**

Friday   Date ..../......./.......

Description	Amount
Total	

Saturday   Date ..../......./.......

Description	Amount
Total	

Sunday   Date ..../......./.......

Description	Amount
Total	

Notes

_____
_____
_____
_____
_____
_____
_____
_____
_____
_____

Weekly Expense Tracker

Month :   Week Of :   Budget :

Monday   Date ..../......./.......

Description	Amount
Total	

Tuesday   Date ..../......./.......

Description	Amount
Total	

Wednesday   Date ..../......./.......

Description	Amount
Total	

Thursday   Date ..../......./.......

Description	Amount
Total	

Weekly Expense Tracker

Total Expenses :   **Balance :**

Friday
Date ....../....../......

Description	Amount
Total	

Saturday
Date ....../....../......

Description	Amount
Total	

Sunday
Date ....../....../......

Description	Amount
Total	

Notes

Weekly Expense Tracker

Month :   Week Of :   Budget :

Monday
Date ....../....../......

Description	Amount
Total	

Tuesday
Date ....../....../......

Description	Amount
Total	

Wednesday
Date ....../....../......

Description	Amount
Total	

Thursday
Date ....../....../......

Description	Amount
Total	

Weekly Expense Tracker

Total Expenses :   Balance :

Friday   Date ..../......./.......

Description	Amount
Total	

Saturday   Date ..../......./.......

Description	Amount
Total	

Sunday   Date ..../......./.......

Description	Amount
Total	

Notes

_____

_____

_____

_____

_____

_____

_____

_____

_____

_____

_____

Weekly Expense Tracker

Month :   Week Of :   Budget :

Monday   Date ..../......./.......

Description	Amount
Total	

Tuesday   Date ..../......./.......

Description	Amount
Total	

Wednesday   Date ..../......./.......

Description	Amount
Total	

Thursday   Date ..../......./.......

Description	Amount
Total	

Weekly Expense Tracker

Total Expenses :   **Balance :**

Friday   Date ....../....../......

Description	Amount
Total	

Saturday   Date ....../....../......

Description	Amount
Total	

Sunday   Date ....../....../......

Description	Amount
Total	

Notes

Monthly Budget

Income		
Income 1		
Income 2		
Other Income		
TOTAL INCOME		

Expenses

Month :

Budget :

Bill To Be Paid	Date Due	Amount	Paid	Note
			◯	
			◯	
			◯	
			◯	
			◯	
			◯	
			◯	
			◯	
			◯	
			◯	
			◯	
			◯	
			◯	
			◯	
			◯	
			◯	
			◯	
			◯	
			◯	
TOTAL				

Monthly Budget

Other Expenses	Date	Amount	Note
TOTAL			

TOTAL INCOME

TOTAL EXPENSES

DIFFERENCE

Notes
_____
_____
_____
_____
_____

Weekly Expense Tracker

Month :   Week Of :   Budget :

Monday   Date ....../....../......

Description	Amount
Total	

Tuesday   Date ....../....../......

Description	Amount
Total	

Wednesday   Date ....../....../......

Description	Amount
Total	

Thursday   Date ....../....../......

Description	Amount
Total	

Weekly Expense Tracker

Total Expenses :   **Balance :**

Friday   Date ..../......./.......

Description	Amount
Total	

Saturday   Date ..../......./.......

Description	Amount
Total	

Sunday   Date ..../......./.......

Description	Amount
Total	

Notes

Weekly Expense Tracker

Month :   **Week Of :**   **Budget :**

Monday   Date ....../....../......

Description	Amount
Total	

Tuesday   Date ....../....../......

Description	Amount
Total	

Wednesday   Date ....../....../......

Description	Amount
Total	

Thursday   Date ....../....../......

Description	Amount
Total	

Weekly Expense Tracker

Total Expenses :   **Balance :**

Friday   Date ..../......./.......

Description	Amount
Total	

Saturday   Date ..../......./.......

Description	Amount
Total	

Sunday   Date ..../......./.......

Description	Amount
Total	

Notes

_____
_____
_____
_____
_____
_____
_____
_____
_____
_____
_____
_____

Weekly Expense Tracker

Month :   Week Of :   Budget :

Monday   Date ..../......./.......

Description	Amount
Total	

Tuesday   Date ..../......./.......

Description	Amount
Total	

Wednesday   Date ..../......./.......

Description	Amount
Total	

Thursday   Date ..../......./.......

Description	Amount
Total	

Weekly Expense Tracker

Total Expenses :   **Balance :**

Friday   Date ..../......./.......

Description	Amount
Total	

Saturday   Date ..../......./.......

Description	Amount
Total	

Sunday   Date ..../......./.......

Description	Amount
Total	

Notes

Weekly Expense Tracker

Month :   Week Of :   Budget :

Monday   Date ..../......./.......

Description	Amount
Total	

Tuesday   Date ..../......./.......

Description	Amount
Total	

Wednesday   Date ..../......./.......

Description	Amount
Total	

Thursday   Date ..../......./.......

Description	Amount
Total	

Weekly Expense Tracker

Total Expenses :   **Balance :**

Friday   Date ..../......./.......

Description	Amount
Total	

Saturday   Date ..../......./.......

Description	Amount
Total	

Sunday   Date ..../......./.......

Description	Amount
Total	

Notes

Weekly Expense Tracker

Month :   Week Of :   Budget :

Monday   Date ..../......./.......

Description	Amount
Total	

Tuesday   Date ..../......./.......

Description	Amount
Total	

Wednesday   Date ..../......./.......

Description	Amount
Total	

Thursday   Date ..../......./.......

Description	Amount
Total	

Weekly Expense Tracker

Total Expenses :   **Balance :**

Friday   Date ..../......./.......

Description	Amount
Total	

Saturday   Date ..../......./.......

Description	Amount
Total	

Sunday   Date ..../......./.......

Description	Amount
Total	

Notes

Monthly Budget

Income		
Income 1		
Income 2		
Other Income		
TOTAL INCOME		

Expenses

Month :

Budget :

Bill To Be Paid	Date Due	Amount	Paid	Note
			○	
			○	
			○	
			○	
			○	
			○	
			○	
			○	
			○	
			○	
			○	
			○	
			○	
			○	
			○	
			○	
			○	
			○	
			○	
TOTAL				

Monthly Budget

Other Expenses	Date	Amount	Note
TOTAL			

TOTAL INCOME

TOTAL EXPENSES

DIFFERENCE

Notes

Weekly Expense Tracker

Month : **Week Of :** **Budget :**

Monday Date ..../......./.......

Description	Amount
Total	

Tuesday Date ..../......./.......

Description	Amount
Total	

Wednesday Date ..../......./.......

Description	Amount
Total	

Thursday Date ..../......./.......

Description	Amount
Total	

Weekly Expense Tracker

Total Expenses :   Balance :

Friday   Date ..../......./.......

Description	Amount
Total	

Saturday   Date ..../......./.......

Description	Amount
Total	

Sunday   Date ..../......./.......

Description	Amount
Total	

Notes

Weekly Expense Tracker

Month :   Week Of :   Budget :

Monday   Date ..../......./.......

Description	Amount
Total	

Tuesday   Date ..../......./.......

Description	Amount
Total	

Wednesday   Date ..../......./.......

Description	Amount
Total	

Thursday   Date ..../......./.......

Description	Amount
Total	

Weekly Expense Tracker

Total Expenses :   **Balance :**

Friday   Date ..../......./.......

Description	Amount
Total	

Saturday   Date ..../......./.......

Description	Amount
Total	

Sunday   Date ..../......./.......

Description	Amount
Total	

Notes

Weekly Expense Tracker

Month :   Week Of :   Budget :

Monday   Date ....../....../......

Description	Amount
Total	

Tuesday   Date ....../....../......

Description	Amount
Total	

Wednesday   Date ....../....../......

Description	Amount
Total	

Thursday   Date ....../....../......

Description	Amount
Total	

Weekly Expense Tracker

Total Expenses :

Balance :

Friday

Date ..../......./.......

Description	Amount
Total	

Saturday

Date ..../......./.......

Description	Amount
Total	

Sunday

Date ..../......./.......

Description	Amount
Total	

Notes

_____
_____
_____
_____
_____
_____
_____
_____
_____
_____

Weekly Expense Tracker

Month :   Week Of :   Budget :

Monday
Date ..../......./.......

Description	Amount
Total	

Tuesday
Date ..../......./.......

Description	Amount
Total	

Wednesday
Date ..../......./.......

Description	Amount
Total	

Thursday
Date ..../......./.......

Description	Amount
Total	

Weekly Expense Tracker

Total Expenses :   **Balance :**

Friday   Date ..../......./.......

Description	Amount
Total	

Saturday   Date ..../......./.......

Description	Amount
Total	

Sunday   Date ..../......./.......

Description	Amount
Total	

Notes

_____
_____
_____
_____
_____
_____
_____
_____
_____

Weekly Expense Tracker

Month :   Week Of :   Budget :

Monday   Date ……/……/……

Description	Amount
Total	

Tuesday   Date ……/……/……

Description	Amount
Total	

Wednesday   Date ……/……/……

Description	Amount
Total	

Thursday   Date ……/……/……

Description	Amount
Total	

Weekly Expense Tracker

Total Expenses :   **Balance :**

Friday   Date ..../......./......

Description	Amount
Total	

Saturday   Date ..../......./......

Description	Amount
Total	

Sunday   Date ..../......./......

Description	Amount
Total	

Notes

_____

_____

_____

_____

_____

_____

_____

_____

_____

_____

_____

Monthly Budget

Income		
Income 1		
Income 2		
Other Income		
TOTAL INCOME		

Expenses

Month :

Budget :

Bill To Be Paid	Date Due	Amount	Paid	Note
			○	
			○	
			○	
			○	
			○	
			○	
			○	
			○	
			○	
			○	
			○	
			○	
			○	
			○	
			○	
			○	
			○	
			○	
TOTAL				

Monthly Budget

Other Expenses	Date	Amount	Note
TOTAL			

TOTAL INCOME

TOTAL EXPENSES

DIFFERENCE

Notes

Weekly Expense Tracker

Month :   Week Of :   Budget :

Monday   Date ....../....../......

Description	Amount
Total	

Tuesday   Date ....../....../......

Description	Amount
Total	

Wednesday   Date ....../....../......

Description	Amount
Total	

Thursday   Date ....../....../......

Description	Amount
Total	

Weekly Expense Tracker

Total Expenses :   **Balance :**

Friday   Date ..../......./.......

Description	Amount
Total	

Saturday   Date ..../......./.......

Description	Amount
Total	

Sunday   Date ..../......./.......

Description	Amount
Total	

Notes

Weekly Expense Tracker

Month :   **Week Of :**   **Budget :**

Monday   Date ..../......./.......

Description	Amount
Total	

Tuesday   Date ..../......./.......

Description	Amount
Total	

Wednesday   Date ..../......./.......

Description	Amount
Total	

Thursday   Date ..../......./.......

Description	Amount
Total	

Weekly Expense Tracker

Total Expenses :   **Balance :**

Friday   Date ..../......./.......

Description	Amount
Total	

Saturday   Date ..../......./.......

Description	Amount
Total	

Sunday   Date ..../......./.......

Description	Amount
Total	

Notes

_____

_____

_____

_____

_____

_____

_____

_____

_____

Weekly Expense Tracker

Month :   Week Of :   Budget :

Monday   Date ..../......./.......

Description	Amount
Total	

Tuesday   Date ..../......./.......

Description	Amount
Total	

Wednesday   Date ..../......./.......

Description	Amount
Total	

Thursday   Date ..../......./.......

Description	Amount
Total	

Weekly Expense Tracker

Total Expenses :   **Balance :**

Friday   Date ..../......./.......

Description	Amount
Total	

Saturday   Date ..../......./.......

Description	Amount
Total	

Sunday   Date ..../......./.......

Description	Amount
Total	

Notes

Weekly Expense Tracker

Month :   Week Of :   Budget :

Monday
Date ....../....../......

Description	Amount
Total	

Tuesday
Date ....../....../......

Description	Amount
Total	

Wednesday
Date ....../....../......

Description	Amount
Total	

Thursday
Date ....../....../......

Description	Amount
Total	

Weekly Expense Tracker

Total Expenses :   **Balance :**

Friday   Date ..../......./.......

Description	Amount
Total	

Saturday   Date ..../......./.......

Description	Amount
Total	

Sunday   Date ..../......./.......

Description	Amount
Total	

Notes

Weekly Expense Tracker

Month :   Week Of :   Budget :

Monday   Date ..../......./.......

Description	Amount
Total	

Tuesday   Date ..../......./.......

Description	Amount
Total	

Wednesday   Date ..../......./.......

Description	Amount
Total	

Thursday   Date ..../......./.......

Description	Amount
Total	

Weekly Expense Tracker

Total Expenses :   **Balance :**

Friday   Date ....../....../......

Description	Amount
Total	

Saturday   Date ....../....../......

Description	Amount
Total	

Sunday   Date ....../....../......

Description	Amount
Total	

Notes

_____
_____
_____
_____
_____
_____
_____
_____
_____
_____

Monthly Budget

Income		
Income 1		
Income 2		
Other Income		
TOTAL INCOME		

Expenses

Month :

Budget :

Bill To Be Paid	Date Due	Amount	Paid	Note
			○	
			○	
			○	
			○	
			○	
			○	
			○	
			○	
			○	
			○	
			○	
			○	
			○	
			○	
			○	
			○	
			○	
			○	
			○	
TOTAL				

Monthly Budget

Other Expenses	Date	Amount	Note
TOTAL			

TOTAL INCOME

TOTAL EXPENSES

DIFFERENCE

Notes

Weekly Expense Tracker

Month :   Week Of :   Budget :

Monday   Date ..../......./.......

Description	Amount
Total	

Tuesday   Date ..../......./.......

Description	Amount
Total	

Wednesday   Date ..../......./.......

Description	Amount
Total	

Thursday   Date ..../......./.......

Description	Amount
Total	

Weekly Expense Tracker

Total Expenses :

Balance :

Friday

Date ....../....../......

Description	Amount
Total	

Saturday

Date ....../....../......

Description	Amount
Total	

Sunday

Date ....../....../......

Description	Amount
Total	

Notes

Weekly Expense Tracker

Month :   Week Of :   Budget :

Monday
Date ..../......./.......

Description	Amount
Total	

Tuesday
Date ..../......./.......

Description	Amount
Total	

Wednesday
Date ..../......./.......

Description	Amount
Total	

Thursday
Date ..../......./.......

Description	Amount
Total	

Weekly Expense Tracker

Total Expenses :   **Balance :**

Friday   Date ….…../….…../….…...

Description	Amount
Total	

Saturday   Date ….…../….…../….…...

Description	Amount
Total	

Sunday   Date ….…../….…../….…...

Description	Amount
Total	

Notes

Weekly Expense Tracker

Month :   Week Of :   Budget :

Monday   Date ..../......./.......

Description	Amount
Total	

Tuesday   Date ..../......./.......

Description	Amount
Total	

Wednesday   Date ..../......./.......

Description	Amount
Total	

Thursday   Date ..../......./.......

Description	Amount
Total	

Weekly Expense Tracker

Total Expenses :   **Balance :**

Friday   Date ..../......./.......

Description	Amount
Total	

Saturday   Date ..../......./.......

Description	Amount
Total	

Sunday   Date ..../......./.......

Description	Amount
Total	

Notes

Weekly Expense Tracker

Month :   **Week Of :**   **Budget :**

Monday   Date ....../....../......

Description	Amount
Total	

Tuesday   Date ....../....../......

Description	Amount
Total	

Wednesday   Date ....../....../......

Description	Amount
Total	

Thursday   Date ....../....../......

Description	Amount
Total	

Weekly Expense Tracker

Total Expenses :　　　　　　　　　　　　　　**Balance :**

Friday　　　Date ....../....../......

Description	Amount
Total	

Saturday　　　Date ....../....../......

Description	Amount
Total	

Sunday　　　Date ....../....../......

Description	Amount
Total	

Notes

_____

_____

_____

_____

_____

_____

_____

_____

_____

_____

Weekly Expense Tracker

Month :   Week Of :   Budget :

Monday   Date ..../......./.......

Description	Amount
Total	

Tuesday   Date ..../......./.......

Description	Amount
Total	

Wednesday   Date ..../......./.......

Description	Amount
Total	

Thursday   Date ..../......./.......

Description	Amount
Total	

Weekly Expense Tracker

Total Expenses :   Balance :

Friday
Date ..../......./.......

Description	Amount
Total	

Saturday
Date ..../......./.......

Description	Amount
Total	

Sunday
Date ..../......./.......

Description	Amount
Total	

Notes

Monthly Budget

Income		
Income 1		
Income 2		
Other Income		
TOTAL INCOME		

Expenses

Month :

Budget :

Bill To Be Paid	Date Due	Amount	Paid	Note
			◯	
			◯	
			◯	
			◯	
			◯	
			◯	
			◯	
			◯	
			◯	
			◯	
			◯	
			◯	
			◯	
			◯	
			◯	
			◯	
			◯	
			◯	
			◯	
TOTAL				

Monthly Budget

Other Expenses	Date	Amount	Note
TOTAL			

TOTAL INCOME

TOTAL EXPENSES

DIFFERENCE

Notes
_____
_____
_____
_____
_____

Weekly Expense Tracker

Month :   Week Of :   Budget :

Monday   Date ..../......./.......

Description	Amount
Total	

Tuesday   Date ..../......./.......

Description	Amount
Total	

Wednesday   Date ..../......./.......

Description	Amount
Total	

Thursday   Date ..../......./.......

Description	Amount
Total	

Weekly Expense Tracker

Total Expenses :   **Balance :**

Friday   Date ..../......./.......

Description	Amount
Total	

Saturday   Date ..../......./.......

Description	Amount
Total	

Sunday   Date ..../......./.......

Description	Amount
Total	

Notes

_____

_____

_____

_____

_____

_____

_____

_____

Weekly Expense Tracker

Month :   Week Of :   Budget :

Monday   Date ..../......./.......

Description	Amount
Total	

Tuesday   Date ..../......./.......

Description	Amount
Total	

Wednesday   Date ..../......./.......

Description	Amount
Total	

Thursday   Date ..../......./.......

Description	Amount
Total	

Weekly Expense Tracker

Total Expenses :   **Balance :**

Friday
Date ..../......./......

Description	Amount
Total	

Saturday
Date ..../......./......

Description	Amount
Total	

Sunday
Date ..../......./......

Description	Amount
Total	

Notes

_____
_____
_____
_____
_____
_____
_____
_____
_____

Weekly Expense Tracker

Month :   Week Of :   Budget :

Monday   Date ..../......./.......

Description	Amount
Total	

Tuesday   Date ..../......./.......

Description	Amount
Total	

Wednesday   Date ..../......./.......

Description	Amount
Total	

Thursday   Date ..../......./.......

Description	Amount
Total	

Weekly Expense Tracker

Total Expenses :   **Balance :**

Friday
Date ..../......./.......

Description	Amount
Total	

Saturday
Date ..../......./.......

Description	Amount
Total	

Sunday
Date ..../......./.......

Description	Amount
Total	

Notes

Weekly Expense Tracker

Month :   Week Of :   Budget :

Monday   Date ....../....../......

Description	Amount
Total	

Tuesday   Date ....../....../......

Description	Amount
Total	

Wednesday   Date ....../....../......

Description	Amount
Total	

Thursday   Date ....../....../......

Description	Amount
Total	

Weekly Expense Tracker

Total Expenses :   **Balance :**

Friday   Date ..../......./.......

Description	Amount
Total	

Saturday   Date ..../......./.......

Description	Amount
Total	

Sunday   Date ..../......./.......

Description	Amount
Total	

Notes

_____

_____

_____

_____

_____

_____

_____

_____

_____

Weekly Expense Tracker

Month :   Week Of :   Budget :

Monday   Date ..../......./.......

Description	Amount
Total	

Tuesday   Date ..../......./.......

Description	Amount
Total	

Wednesday   Date ..../......./.......

Description	Amount
Total	

Thursday   Date ..../......./.......

Description	Amount
Total	

Weekly Expense Tracker

Total Expenses :   **Balance :**

Friday   Date ..../......./.......

Description	Amount
Total	

Saturday   Date ..../......./.......

Description	Amount
Total	

Sunday   Date ..../......./.......

Description	Amount
Total	

Notes

_____

_____

_____

_____

_____

_____

_____

_____

_____

_____

Monthly Budget

Income		
Income 1		
Income 2		
Other Income		
TOTAL INCOME		

Expenses

Month :

Budget :

Bill To Be Paid	Date Due	Amount	Paid	Note
			○	
			○	
			○	
			○	
			○	
			○	
			○	
			○	
			○	
			○	
			○	
			○	
			○	
			○	
			○	
			○	
			○	
			○	
			○	
TOTAL				

Monthly Budget

Other Expenses	Date	Amount	Note
TOTAL			

TOTAL INCOME

TOTAL EXPENSES

DIFFERENCE

Notes

_____

_____

_____

_____

_____

Weekly Expense Tracker

Month :   Week Of :   Budget :

Monday   Date ....../....../......

Description	Amount
Total	

Tuesday   Date ....../....../......

Description	Amount
Total	

Wednesday   Date ....../....../......

Description	Amount
Total	

Thursday   Date ....../....../......

Description	Amount
Total	

Weekly Expense Tracker

Total Expenses :   **Balance :**

Friday   Date ..../......./.......

Description	Amount
Total	

Saturday   Date ..../......./.......

Description	Amount
Total	

Sunday   Date ..../......./.......

Description	Amount
Total	

Notes

Weekly Expense Tracker

Month :   Week Of :   Budget :

Monday   Date ..../......./.......

Description	Amount
Total	

Tuesday   Date ..../......./.......

Description	Amount
Total	

Wednesday   Date ..../......./.......

Description	Amount
Total	

Thursday   Date ..../......./.......

Description	Amount
Total	

Weekly Expense Tracker

Total Expenses :   **Balance :**

Friday   Date …...../…...../…......

Description	Amount
Total	

Saturday   Date …...../…...../…......

Description	Amount
Total	

Sunday   Date …...../…...../…......

Description	Amount
Total	

Notes

Weekly Expense Tracker

Month :   Week Of :   Budget :

Monday   Date ..../......./.......

Description	Amount
Total	

Tuesday   Date ..../......./.......

Description	Amount
Total	

Wednesday   Date ..../......./.......

Description	Amount
Total	

Thursday   Date ..../......./.......

Description	Amount
Total	

Weekly Expense Tracker

Total Expenses :   **Balance :**

Friday   Date ....../....../......

Description	Amount
Total	

Saturday   Date ....../....../......

Description	Amount
Total	

Sunday   Date ....../....../......

Description	Amount
Total	

Notes

Weekly Expense Tracker

Month :　　　　　　　　**Week Of :**　　　　　　　　**Budget :**

Monday　　Date ..../......./.......

Description	Amount
Total	

Tuesday　　Date ..../......./.......

Description	Amount
Total	

Wednesday　　Date ..../......./.......

Description	Amount
Total	

Thursday　　Date ..../......./.......

Description	Amount
Total	

Weekly Expense Tracker

Total Expenses :   **Balance :**

Friday   Date …...../…...../…......

Description	Amount
Total	

Saturday   Date …...../…...../…......

Description	Amount
Total	

Sunday   Date …...../…...../…......

Description	Amount
Total	

Notes

_____

_____

_____

_____

_____

_____

_____

_____

_____

Weekly Expense Tracker

Month :   Week Of :   Budget :

Monday   Date ....../....../......

Description	Amount
Total	

Tuesday   Date ....../....../......

Description	Amount
Total	

Wednesday   Date ....../....../......

Description	Amount
Total	

Thursday   Date ....../....../......

Description	Amount
Total	

Weekly Expense Tracker

Total Expenses :   **Balance :**

Friday   Date ……/……/……

Description	Amount
Total	

Saturday   Date ……/……/……

Description	Amount
Total	

Sunday   Date ……/……/……

Description	Amount
Total	

Notes

Monthly Budget

Income		
Income 1		
Income 2		
Other Income		
TOTAL INCOME		

Expenses

Month :

Budget :

Bill To Be Paid	Date Due	Amount	Paid	Note
			○	
			○	
			○	
			○	
			○	
			○	
			○	
			○	
			○	
			○	
			○	
			○	
			○	
			○	
			○	
			○	
			○	
			○	
TOTAL				

Monthly Budget

Other Expenses	Date	Amount	Note
TOTAL			

TOTAL INCOME

TOTAL EXPENSES

DIFFERENCE

Notes

_____

_____

_____

_____

_____

Weekly Expense Tracker

Month :   Week Of :   Budget :

Monday   Date ..../......./.......

Description	Amount
Total	

Tuesday   Date ..../......./.......

Description	Amount
Total	

Wednesday   Date ..../......./.......

Description	Amount
Total	

Thursday   Date ..../......./.......

Description	Amount
Total	

Weekly Expense Tracker

Total Expenses :   **Balance :**

Friday   Date ..../......./.......

Description	Amount
Total	

Saturday   Date ..../......./.......

Description	Amount
Total	

Sunday   Date ..../......./.......

Description	Amount
Total	

Notes

_____
_____
_____
_____
_____
_____
_____
_____
_____

Weekly Expense Tracker

Month :   Week Of :   Budget :

Monday   Date ..../......./.......

Description	Amount
Total	

Tuesday   Date ..../......./.......

Description	Amount
Total	

Wednesday   Date ..../......./.......

Description	Amount
Total	

Thursday   Date ..../......./.......

Description	Amount
Total	

Weekly Expense Tracker

Total Expenses :   Balance :

Friday   Date ..../......./.......

Description	Amount
Total	

Saturday   Date ..../......./.......

Description	Amount
Total	

Sunday   Date ..../......./.......

Description	Amount
Total	

Notes

Weekly Expense Tracker

Month :   **Week Of :**   **Budget :**

Monday   Date ....../....../......

Description	Amount
Total	

Tuesday   Date ....../....../......

Description	Amount
Total	

Wednesday   Date ....../....../......

Description	Amount
Total	

Thursday   Date ....../....../......

Description	Amount
Total	

Weekly Expense Tracker

Total Expenses :   **Balance :**

Friday   Date ..../......./.......

Description	Amount
Total	

Saturday   Date ..../......./.......

Description	Amount
Total	

Sunday   Date ..../......./.......

Description	Amount
Total	

Notes

_____

_____

_____

_____

_____

_____

_____

_____

_____

Weekly Expense Tracker

Month :   Week Of :   Budget :

Monday
Date ....../....../......

Description	Amount
Total	

Tuesday
Date ....../....../......

Description	Amount
Total	

Wednesday
Date ....../....../......

Description	Amount
Total	

Thursday
Date ....../....../......

Description	Amount
Total	

Weekly Expense Tracker

Total Expenses :   **Balance :**

Friday   Date ..../......./.......

Description	Amount
Total	

Saturday   Date ..../......./.......

Description	Amount
Total	

Sunday   Date ..../......./.......

Description	Amount
Total	

Notes

Weekly Expense Tracker

Month :   Week Of :   Budget :

Monday
Date ..../......./.......

Description	Amount
Total	

Tuesday
Date ..../......./.......

Description	Amount
Total	

Wednesday
Date ..../......./.......

Description	Amount
Total	

Thursday
Date ..../......./.......

Description	Amount
Total	

Weekly Expense Tracker

Total Expenses :   **Balance :**

Friday   Date ..../......./.......

Description	Amount
Total	

Saturday   Date ..../......./.......

Description	Amount
Total	

Sunday   Date ..../......./.......

Description	Amount
Total	

Notes

Monthly Budget

Income		
Income 1		
Income 2		
Other Income		
TOTAL INCOME		

Expenses

Month :

Budget :

Bill To Be Paid	Date Due	Amount	Paid	Note
			◯	
			◯	
			◯	
			◯	
			◯	
			◯	
			◯	
			◯	
			◯	
			◯	
			◯	
			◯	
			◯	
			◯	
			◯	
			◯	
			◯	
			◯	
			◯	
TOTAL				

Monthly Budget

Other Expenses	Date	Amount	Note
TOTAL			

TOTAL INCOME

TOTAL EXPENSES

DIFFERENCE

Notes

Weekly Expense Tracker

Month :   **Week Of :**   **Budget :**

Monday   Date ..../......./.......

Description	Amount
Total	

Tuesday   Date ..../......./.......

Description	Amount
Total	

Wednesday   Date ..../......./.......

Description	Amount
Total	

Thursday   Date ..../......./.......

Description	Amount
Total	

Weekly Expense Tracker

Total Expenses :   **Balance :**

Friday   Date ....../....../......

Description	Amount
Total	

Saturday   Date ....../....../......

Description	Amount
Total	

Sunday   Date ....../....../......

Description	Amount
Total	

Notes

Weekly Expense Tracker

Month :   Week Of :   Budget :

Monday   Date ....../....../......

Description	Amount
Total	

Tuesday   Date ....../....../......

Description	Amount
Total	

Wednesday   Date ....../....../......

Description	Amount
Total	

Thursday   Date ....../....../......

Description	Amount
Total	

Weekly Expense Tracker

Total Expenses :   **Balance :**

Friday
Date ....../....../......

Description	Amount
Total	

Saturday
Date ....../....../......

Description	Amount
Total	

Sunday
Date ....../....../......

Description	Amount
Total	

Notes

Weekly Expense Tracker

Month :   Week Of :   Budget :

Monday

Date ..../......./.......

Description	Amount
Total	

Tuesday

Date ..../......./.......

Description	Amount
Total	

Wednesday

Date ..../......./.......

Description	Amount
Total	

Thursday

Date ..../......./.......

Description	Amount
Total	

Weekly Expense Tracker

Total Expenses :   **Balance :**

Friday   Date ….…/….…/….…

Description	Amount
Total	

Saturday   Date ….…/….…/….…

Description	Amount
Total	

Sunday   Date ….…/….…/….…

Description	Amount
Total	

Notes

_____
_____
_____
_____
_____
_____
_____
_____
_____

Weekly Expense Tracker

Month :   Week Of :   Budget :

Monday   Date ..../......./.......

Description	Amount
Total	

Tuesday   Date ..../......./.......

Description	Amount
Total	

Wednesday   Date ..../......./.......

Description	Amount
Total	

Thursday   Date ..../......./.......

Description	Amount
Total	

Weekly Expense Tracker

Total Expenses :   **Balance :**

Friday   Date ..../......./.......

Description	Amount
Total	

Saturday   Date ..../......./.......

Description	Amount
Total	

Sunday   Date ..../......./.......

Description	Amount
Total	

Notes

_____
_____
_____
_____
_____
_____
_____
_____
_____
_____
_____

Weekly Expense Tracker

Month :   Week Of :   Budget :

Monday   Date ..../......./.......

Description	Amount
Total	

Tuesday   Date ..../......./.......

Description	Amount
Total	

Wednesday   Date ..../......./.......

Description	Amount
Total	

Thursday   Date ..../......./.......

Description	Amount
Total	

Weekly Expense Tracker

Total Expenses :   **Balance :**

Friday   Date ..../......./.......

Description	Amount
Total	

Saturday   Date ..../......./.......

Description	Amount
Total	

Sunday   Date ..../......./.......

Description	Amount
Total	

Notes

Monthly Budget

Income		
Income 1		
Income 2		
Other Income		
TOTAL INCOME		

Expenses

Month :

Budget :

Bill To Be Paid	Date Due	Amount	Paid	Note
			◯	
			◯	
			◯	
			◯	
			◯	
			◯	
			◯	
			◯	
			◯	
			◯	
			◯	
			◯	
			◯	
			◯	
			◯	
			◯	
			◯	
			◯	
			◯	
TOTAL				

Monthly Budget

Other Expenses	Date	Amount	Note
TOTAL			

TOTAL INCOME

TOTAL EXPENSES

DIFFERENCE

Notes
_____
_____
_____
_____
_____

Weekly Expense Tracker

Month :   Week Of :   Budget :

Monday   Date ....../....../......

Description	Amount
Total	

Tuesday   Date ....../....../......

Description	Amount
Total	

Wednesday   Date ....../....../......

Description	Amount
Total	

Thursday   Date ....../....../......

Description	Amount
Total	

Weekly Expense Tracker

Total Expenses :   **Balance :**

Friday   Date ....../....../......

Description	Amount
Total	

Saturday   Date ....../....../......

Description	Amount
Total	

Sunday   Date ....../....../......

Description	Amount
Total	

Notes

_____
_____
_____
_____
_____
_____
_____
_____

Weekly Expense Tracker

Month :   Week Of :   Budget :

Monday   Date ..../......./.......

Description	Amount
Total	

Tuesday   Date ..../......./.......

Description	Amount
Total	

Wednesday   Date ..../......./.......

Description	Amount
Total	

Thursday   Date ..../......./.......

Description	Amount
Total	

Weekly Expense Tracker

Total Expenses :   **Balance :**

Friday   Date ..../......./.......

Description	Amount
Total	

Saturday   Date ..../......./.......

Description	Amount
Total	

Sunday   Date ..../......./.......

Description	Amount
Total	

Notes

Weekly Expense Tracker

Month :   Week Of :   Budget :

Monday   Date ..../......./.......

Description	Amount
Total	

Tuesday   Date ..../......./.......

Description	Amount
Total	

Wednesday   Date ..../......./.......

Description	Amount
Total	

Thursday   Date ..../......./.......

Description	Amount
Total	

Weekly Expense Tracker

Total Expenses :   **Balance :**

Friday   Date ….…/….…/….…

Description	Amount
Total	

Saturday   Date ….…/….…/….…

Description	Amount
Total	

Sunday   Date ….…/….…/….…

Description	Amount
Total	

Notes

Weekly Expense Tracker

Month :   Week Of :   Budget :

Monday   Date ....../....../......

Description	Amount
Total	

Tuesday   Date ....../....../......

Description	Amount
Total	

Wednesday   Date ....../....../......

Description	Amount
Total	

Thursday   Date ....../....../......

Description	Amount
Total	

Weekly Expense Tracker

Total Expenses :   **Balance :**

Friday   Date ..../......./.......

Description	Amount
Total	

Saturday   Date ..../......./.......

Description	Amount
Total	

Sunday   Date ..../......./.......

Description	Amount
Total	

Notes

Weekly Expense Tracker

Month :   Week Of :   Budget :

Monday   Date ..../......./.......

Description	Amount
Total	

Tuesday   Date ..../......./.......

Description	Amount
Total	

Wednesday   Date ..../......./.......

Description	Amount
Total	

Thursday   Date ..../......./.......

Description	Amount
Total	

Weekly Expense Tracker

Total Expenses :   **Balance :**

Friday   Date ....../....../......

Description	Amount
Total	

Saturday   Date ....../....../......

Description	Amount
Total	

Sunday   Date ....../....../......

Description	Amount
Total	

Notes

_____

_____

_____

_____

_____

_____

_____

_____

_____

Monthly Budget

Income		
Income 1		
Income 2		
Other Income		
TOTAL INCOME		

Expenses

Month :

Budget :

Bill To Be Paid	Date Due	Amount	Paid	Note
			◯	
			◯	
			◯	
			◯	
			◯	
			◯	
			◯	
			◯	
			◯	
			◯	
			◯	
			◯	
			◯	
			◯	
			◯	
			◯	
			◯	
			◯	
TOTAL				

Monthly Budget

Other Expenses	Date	Amount	Note
TOTAL			

TOTAL INCOME

TOTAL EXPENSES

DIFFERENCE

Notes
_____
_____
_____
_____
_____

Weekly Expense Tracker

Month : **Week Of :** **Budget :**

Monday
Date ....../....../......

Description	Amount
Total	

Tuesday
Date ....../....../......

Description	Amount
Total	

Wednesday
Date ....../....../......

Description	Amount
Total	

Thursday
Date ....../....../......

Description	Amount
Total	

Weekly Expense Tracker

Total Expenses :   **Balance :**

Friday   Date ..../......./.......

Description	Amount
Total	

Saturday   Date ..../......./.......

Description	Amount
Total	

Sunday   Date ..../......./.......

Description	Amount
Total	

Notes

_____

_____

_____

_____

_____

_____

_____

_____

_____

Weekly Expense Tracker

Month : **Week Of :** **Budget :**

Monday Date ..../......./.......

Description	Amount
Total	

Tuesday Date ..../......./.......

Description	Amount
Total	

Wednesday Date ..../......./.......

Description	Amount
Total	

Thursday Date ..../......./.......

Description	Amount
Total	

Weekly Expense Tracker

Total Expenses :   Balance :

Friday   Date ....../....../......

Description	Amount
Total	

Saturday   Date ....../....../......

Description	Amount
Total	

Sunday   Date ....../....../......

Description	Amount
Total	

Notes

Weekly Expense Tracker

Month :   Week Of :   Budget :

Monday   Date ....../....../......

Description	Amount
Total	

Tuesday   Date ....../....../......

Description	Amount
Total	

Wednesday   Date ....../....../......

Description	Amount
Total	

Thursday   Date ....../....../......

Description	Amount
Total	

Weekly Expense Tracker

Total Expenses :   **Balance :**

Friday   Date ..../......./.......

Description	Amount
Total	

Saturday   Date ..../......./.......

Description	Amount
Total	

Sunday   Date ..../......./.......

Description	Amount
Total	

Notes

Weekly Expense Tracker

Month :   Week Of :   Budget :

Monday   Date ....../....../......

Description	Amount
Total	

Tuesday   Date ....../....../......

Description	Amount
Total	

Wednesday   Date ....../....../......

Description	Amount
Total	

Thursday   Date ....../....../......

Description	Amount
Total	

Weekly Expense Tracker

Total Expenses :   **Balance :**

Friday   Date ..../......./.......

Description	Amount
Total	

Saturday   Date ..../......./.......

Description	Amount
Total	

Sunday   Date ..../......./.......

Description	Amount
Total	

Notes

Weekly Expense Tracker

Month :   **Week Of :**   **Budget :**

Monday   Date ....../....../......

Description	Amount
Total	

Tuesday   Date ....../....../......

Description	Amount
Total	

Wednesday   Date ....../....../......

Description	Amount
Total	

Thursday   Date ....../....../......

Description	Amount
Total	

Weekly Expense Tracker

Total Expenses :   **Balance :**

Friday   Date ....../....../......

Description	Amount
Total	

Saturday   Date ....../....../......

Description	Amount
Total	

Sunday   Date ....../....../......

Description	Amount
Total	

Notes

Monthly Budget

Income		
Income 1		
Income 2		
Other Income		
TOTAL INCOME		

Expenses

Month :

Budget :

Bill To Be Paid	Date Due	Amount	Paid	Note
			◯	
			◯	
			◯	
			◯	
			◯	
			◯	
			◯	
			◯	
			◯	
			◯	
			◯	
			◯	
			◯	
			◯	
			◯	
			◯	
			◯	
			◯	
TOTAL				

Monthly Budget

Other Expenses	Date	Amount	Note
TOTAL			

TOTAL INCOME

TOTAL EXPENSES

DIFFERENCE

Notes

Weekly Expense Tracker

Month :   Week Of :   Budget :

Monday   Date ..../......./.......

Description	Amount
Total	

Tuesday   Date ..../......./.......

Description	Amount
Total	

Wednesday   Date ..../......./.......

Description	Amount
Total	

Thursday   Date ..../......./.......

Description	Amount
Total	

Weekly Expense Tracker

Total Expenses :   **Balance :**

Friday   Date ..../......./.......

Description	Amount
Total	

Saturday   Date ..../......./.......

Description	Amount
Total	

Sunday   Date ..../......./.......

Description	Amount
Total	

Notes

Weekly Expense Tracker

Month :   Week Of :   Budget :

Monday
Date ..../......./.......

Description	Amount
Total	

Tuesday
Date ..../......./.......

Description	Amount
Total	

Wednesday
Date ..../......./.......

Description	Amount
Total	

Thursday
Date ..../......./.......

Description	Amount
Total	

Weekly Expense Tracker

Total Expenses :   **Balance :**

Friday
Date ....../....../......

Description	Amount
Total	

Saturday
Date ....../....../......

Description	Amount
Total	

Sunday
Date ....../....../......

Description	Amount
Total	

Notes

Weekly Expense Tracker

Month :   **Week Of :**   **Budget :**

Monday   Date ……/……/……

Description	Amount
Total	

Tuesday   Date ……/……/……

Description	Amount
Total	

Wednesday   Date ……/……/……

Description	Amount
Total	

Thursday   Date ……/……/……

Description	Amount
Total	

Weekly Expense Tracker

Total Expenses :   **Balance :**

Friday   Date …..../…..../…....

Description	Amount
Total	

Saturday   Date …..../…..../…....

Description	Amount
Total	

Sunday   Date …..../…..../…....

Description	Amount
Total	

Notes

Weekly Expense Tracker

Month :   Week Of :   Budget :

Monday   Date ..../......./.......

Description	Amount
Total	

Tuesday   Date ..../......./.......

Description	Amount
Total	

Wednesday   Date ..../......./.......

Description	Amount
Total	

Thursday   Date ..../......./.......

Description	Amount
Total	

Weekly Expense Tracker

Total Expenses :   Balance :

Friday   Date ..../......./.......

Description	Amount
Total	

Saturday   Date ..../......./.......

Description	Amount
Total	

Sunday   Date ..../......./.......

Description	Amount
Total	

Notes

Weekly Expense Tracker

Month :   Week Of :   Budget :

Monday   Date ..../......./.......

Description	Amount
Total	

Tuesday   Date ..../......./.......

Description	Amount
Total	

Wednesday   Date ..../......./.......

Description	Amount
Total	

Thursday   Date ..../......./.......

Description	Amount
Total	

Weekly Expense Tracker

Total Expenses :   **Balance :**

Friday
Date ..../......./.......

Description	Amount
Total	

Saturday
Date ..../......./.......

Description	Amount
Total	

Sunday
Date ..../......./.......

Description	Amount
Total	

Notes

Notes

Made in the USA
Las Vegas, NV
04 January 2022

40341602R00083